This book is for
my pug dog
CHIPPENDALE,
who loves cars
still more than I do.

Huck Scarry

ON THE ROAD

First published 1981
Published in the United States of America by
Philomel Books, a division of
the Putnam Publishing Group, New York

ISBN 0-399-20818-6 (TB)
ISBN 0-399-61183-5 (GB)
Co-edition arranged with the help of Angus Hudson, London

PHILOMEL
BOOKS

New York

Gasoline-powered wagon
of Siegfried Marcus,
Austria,
late
1800s

Gottlieb Daimler's
horseless carriage,
Germany, 1886

Saddle

Carl Benz's
motorized tricycle,
Germany, 1885

The Danish
Hammel car, 1887

Daimler motorcycle,
Germany, 1885

The French
Panhard-Levassor
used a Daimler engine
mounted up front,
1891

"La Mancelle,"
the steam-powered
carriage of
Amédée Bollée, France, 1878

A
Panhard-Levassor
truck, 1893

Only one hundred
years ago, there were no cars.
For long trips, one took the train.
Otherwise, people got about on horseback
or, more comfortably,
in a carriage pulled by a horse.

However, imaginative inventors
in many lands tried putting
small motors onto carriages.
Now the carriages could move
by themselves, so these new inventions
were called "Automobiles!"

The Australian "Pioneer" of 1898

These early automobiles were very different from the ones we drive today. See how many shapes and sizes there were! Some cars ran on steam power, like railway locomotives, and others made use of the newly invented gasoline engine.
Peter Pebble joins the cars that drove the dusty roads of times gone by. He's off!

The First Renault France, 1898

Motorized tricycle of Léon Bollée, France, 1895

Robinia tree

This Scotte steam bus could go only 5 miles per hour, France, 1892

The first American car was probably the Duryea of 1893

Henry Ford's first car, built in 1896

5

Henry Ford's racer, the "No. 999" capable of driving 100 MPH! (USA, 1902)

Spark arrester

Camille Jenatzy's electric car, "La Jamais Contente." The fastest on earth in 1889, driving 60 MPH (France)

Emile Levassor's No. 5, winner of the Paris-Bordeaux-Paris race of 1895. Average speed: 15 MPH

Amédée Bollée's steam bus, "La Nouvelle", of 1880, took part in the Paris-Bordeaux race of 1895

Boiler

LIVRAISON A DOMICILE

BELLE JARDINIÈRE

Leblant delivery truck, 1894

A De Dion steam car, winner of the world's first race from Paris, France, to Rouen, 1894. Average speed: 10 MPH

No sooner did people have cars to drive, than they began to race them. Races showed which cars were fastest and most reliable.

The first races were held on public roads, between cities.

Spectators lined the roadside to cheer on the speeding cars.

The **New York Herald** *newspaper sponsored the Gordon Bennett Races, offering big prizes. Here are some winners:*

1900, Fernand Charron, France

1902, Marcel Renault, France

1903, Camille Jenatzy in a Mercedes, Germany

1904, 1905, Léon Théry, in a Brasier, France

Detachable planks to bridge streams

Robust Trans-continental racers

Big gasoline tanks

The 1907 Thomas "Flyer" drove westwards from New York Paris, France (with some help over the ocean, of course)!

This 1907 Itala drove from Peking, China to Paris, France

7

Grand Prix racers: 1906–1914

1908 Austin racer,
England

The 1908 Grand Prix
was won by
Christian Lautenschläger,
in a Mercedes

The "Blitzen Benz,"
Germany, 1909

The first Grand Prix race
was held at Le Mans, France,
in 1906. François Szisz
was the winner
in this Renault

Felice Nazzaro
won the 1907 Grand Prix
in this Fiat

Big gasoline tank

Driver's seat
Mechanic's seat

1906 Locomobile,
winner of the 1908
Vanderbilt Race (USA)

Here is a Grand Prix race!
Powerful cars from many lands
battle with speed to win first prize.

Peter Pebble is moving quickly into
last place, but he has been rewarded
with a rubber wreath just the same!

*Giant Fiat
300 CV racer
Italy, 1910*

MICHELIN MICHELIN

*An Italian
Aquila Italiana
of 1912*

Spare tires

*A French Peugeot
won the Grand Prix
of 1912 and 1913,
driven by
Georges Boillot*

*Christian Lautenschläger
drove his Mercedes into
first place in the 1914
Grand Prix (Germany)*

*A quick change
of tires*

A 1908 Benz racer

American cars and trucks: 1900–1913

Mirror →

The speedway at Indianapolis, Indiana was opened in 1909, and paved with over 3 million bricks!

Ray Harroun won the first Indianapolis 500 mile race in 1911, in the Marmon Wasp

The 1912 National racer

In 1903, a Cadillac looked much like a Ford!

Detachable rear seats

1911 Indian motorcycle

1903 Cadillac

Ford Model A of 1903

1913 Harley-Davidson motorcycle

Peter Pebble drives a popular Ford Model T of 1908

The 1902 Holsman was an all-terrain horseless buggy

The First Oldsmobile, 1900

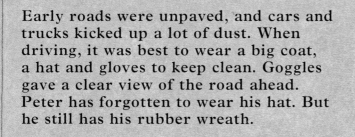

Early roads were unpaved, and cars and trucks kicked up a lot of dust. When driving, it was best to wear a big coat, a hat and gloves to keep clean. Goggles gave a clear view of the road ahead. Peter has forgotten to wear his hat. But he still has his rubber wreath.

White "O Type" steamer, 1909

Big spotlight

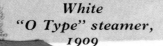

1912 GMC Reliance truck

Dashing Mercer Raceabout, 1913

Buick Model C, 1905

Pierce-Arrow flatbed truck, 1913

Balance Wheel →

The unusual Scripps Booth "Bi-Autogo" cyclecar, 1913

Cars and trucks from Europe: 1900–1913

Not a hatbox, but a box for the spare tire

Brillié-Schneider bus, Paris, France, 1906

MONTMARTRE St GERMAIN des PRES

Place Clichy · OPÉRA · Palais Royal

COMPAGNIE GENERALE DES OMNIBUS

1903 Mercedes limousine, Germany

De Dion-Bouton 8 of 1904, France

1901 Daimler Mercedes, Germany

Hispano-Suiza coupé de ville of 1910, Spain

A propeller-powered motorcycle, France, 1906

One of the first F.I.A.T.s (Fabbrica Italiana di Automobili, Torino) Italy, 1900

Bareheaded
butler

"BANG!" comes a jolt from under
Peter's car. He pulls over to the
curb to see what is wrong. Alas,
a tire has a puncture and needs
to be changed.
Luckily, Peter has a spare one!

1913 Delahaye
landaulette,
France

Opening   windshield

Folding top

Flat tires were the early
motorist's No. 1 enemy

Trolley
pylon

Jack   Tools   Compressed
air can

A car with elastic wheels
France, 1906

Ettore Bugatti
designed this
"Baby" Peugeot
in 1911, France

Painter

Paver

1906 Renault
touring berline

Rail joint

Ladder

Trolley rails

Paving stones

Sand

1903 Fiat flatbed truck

Paver's
stool
and hammer

British cars and trucks: 1895–1914

THE UPPIN ARMS

Hotel

Impolite porter

Disturbed doorman

Thornycroft steam van, 1896

Lamppost

Horse-drawn street sweeper

Litter

A flat hat

British horse-drawn hansom cab

1900 Singer tricycle

1903 Vauxhall

"Motor Wheel"

1908 Leyland truck

Biscuits

B. SQUEE

U.P.&Cº CALCUTTA

T.C.S. RANGOON

K.S.C. HONG KONG

K.S.C. BOMBAY

M.S.A. PENANG

SINGAPORE

K.S.C. BANGKOK

APNM YLOILO

PCC RANGOON

F.S. BOUGY

K.S.C. BOMBAY

M.S.A. PENANG

Tandem racing bicycle, 1895

1902 Holden motorcycle and trailer

Rolls Royce Silver Ghost, 1907

14

1912 Aberdonia landau de ville

In Great Britain, until 1896 cars had to be preceded by a man carrying a red flag

Trolley arm picking up electric current from the overhead wire

Ticket ← dispenser

Glaswegian trolley conductress (1914)

1910 Lanchester

TOLLCROSS PARKHEAD AND PAISLEY Rᴰ

GLASGOW CORPORATION

1909 Dennis Mailvan

Royal Mail.

Doubledecker trolley car, Glasgow, 1898

1905 Lagonda tricycle

Cars and trucks rumble over the cobblestones on the city street. "DRING! Dring! DRING!" goes the bell of the trolley car as it glides along the rails. A good view can be had from the upper deck, but you must hold onto your hat.

Humber motorcycle, 1901

Governess pushing a baby carriage

Pushcart

DRAPERS

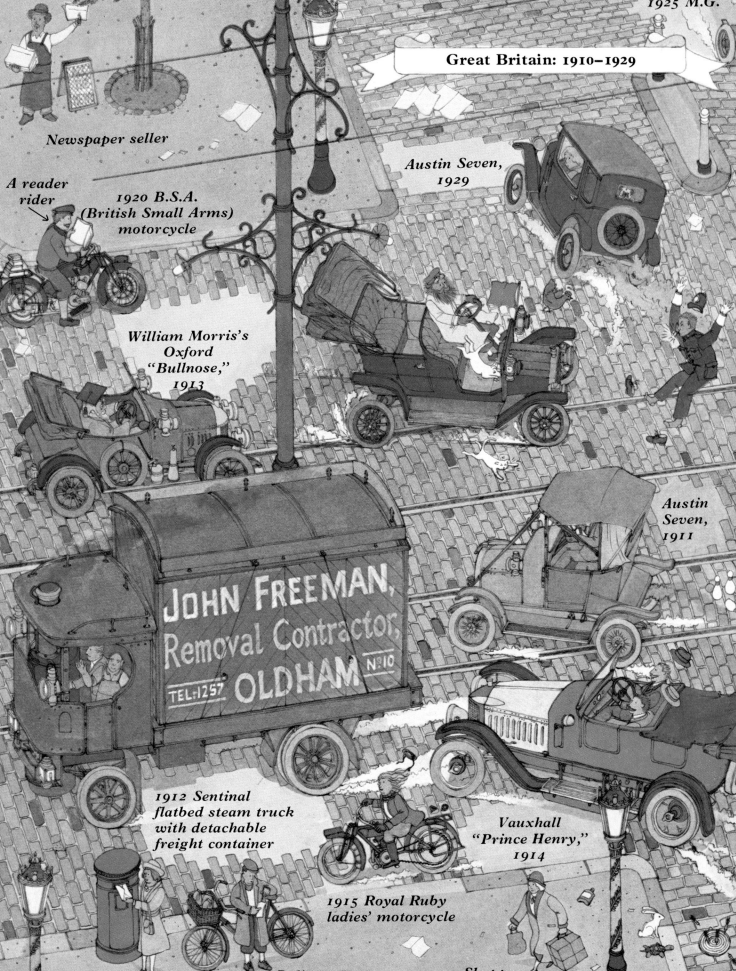

1925 M.G.

Newspaper seller

A reader rider

1920 B.S.A. (British Small Arms) motorcycle

Austin Seven, 1929

William Morris's Oxford "Bullnose," 1913

Austin Seven, 1911

JOHN FREEMAN, Removal Contractor, OLDHAM Nº 10 TEL. 1257

1912 Sentinal flatbed steam truck with detachable freight container

Vauxhall "Prince Henry," 1914

1915 Royal Ruby ladies' motorcycle

16   Mailbox   Delivery Boy   Shopper

Three-wheeled London taxi, 1929

"TWEET!" sounds the policeman's whistle. "SCREECH!" answer the tires of Peter Pebble's car as Peter brakes to an abrupt halt. At a busy intersection drivers must obey the policeman's signals as he guides the traffic safely by.

A girls' school outing

1914 AC "Sociable"

TRY "TY·PHOO" TEA for Indigestion

British Daimler limousine, 1913

AEC K Class London bus, 1920

1914 Albion truck

Manhole

1923 Scott "Squirrel"

Patient pedestrian

1921 Economic

Policeman

Bagpipes

Nasty pickpocket

Pedestrian crossing

1914 Morgan cyclecar

Poor beggar

Traffic island

Gutter

Generous gentleman

17

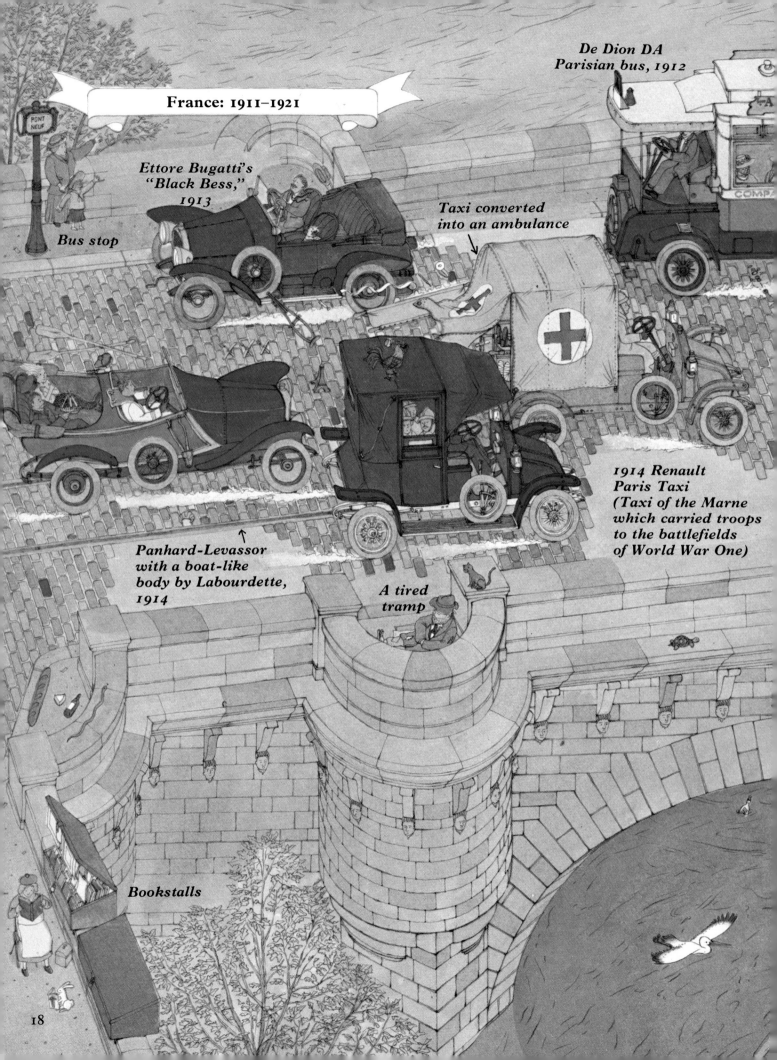

PONT NEUF

Ettore Bugatti's "Black Bess," 1913

Taxi converted into an ambulance

De Dion DA Parisian bus, 1912

Bus stop

1914 Renault Paris Taxi (Taxi of the Marne which carried troops to the battlefields of World War One)

Panhard-Levassor with a boat-like body by Labourdette, 1914

A tired tramp

Bookstalls

18

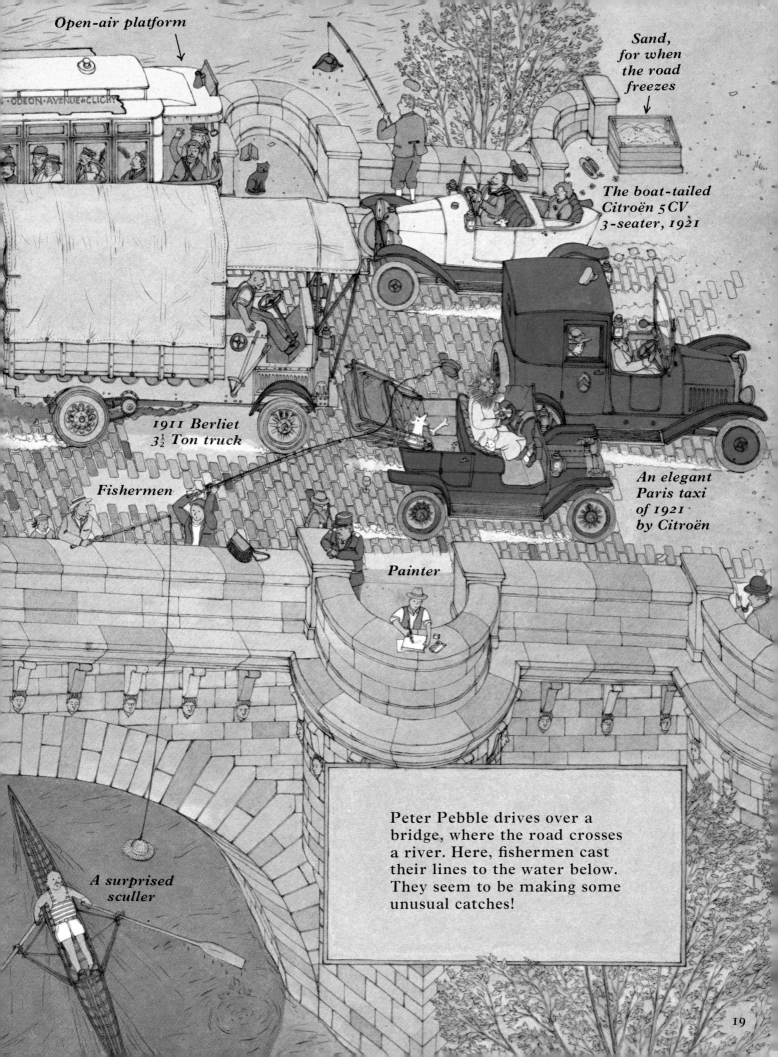

Open-air platform

Sand, for when the road freezes

ODEON·AVENUE·CLICHY

The boat-tailed Citroën 5 CV 3-seater, 1921

1911 Berliet 3½ Ton truck

Fishermen

An elegant Paris taxi of 1921 by Citroën

Painter

A surprised sculler

Peter Pebble drives over a bridge, where the road crosses a river. Here, fishermen cast their lines to the water below. They seem to be making some unusual catches!

1910 Saurer
Royal Bavarian postal bus

Speed limit
sign

Kilometer
marker

Curbstones

Hiker

Potholes

Gas tank
cap

Aerodynamic Rumpler
"Teardrop" car of 1921

Swiss Tribelhorn
3-wheeler, 1919

The Hanomag "Kommissbrot"
looked like a loaf of
pumpernickel bread! 1924

Rotary engine

1922 Megola
motorcycle

The landscape darkens as
rainclouds cover the sky.
"Plink, Plunk, Plink!" sound
the raindrops as they fall on
Peter's head.

Peter pulls off the road to
put up the top.

"Road narrows" sign

Swiss Fischer torpedo tourer, 1913

Audi "Alpensieger," 1914

Luggage trunk

Swiss Motosacoche motorcycle, 1927

PILLON

Swiss Saurer postal bus of 1920, carrying passengers and mail to remote alpine valleys

Clammy campers

Leaky tent

21

Carl A. Neracher's Ner-A-Car motorcycle, 1925

Loose shingles

Tarpaulin

Four-wheel drive Jeffrey Quad, 1915

A diver driver

NUSSBAUM LUMBER CO.

Chevrolet 490 of 1916

A stick in the mud

1912 Oakland

Waiting for help

The rain has turned the white, dusty road into a brown mire of mud!

Some unlucky cars have become trapped in the sticky mess, and wait for help to pull them out.

Peter had better not stop here, for he'd get stuck.

Rumble seat

A silent Detroit electric car, 1917

1921 Automatic electric car

1922 Wills Sainte Claire

1921 Ford Model T saloon

1924 Harley-Davidson motorcycle and sidecar

The 1911 Reeves "Octoauto" had three steering axles

Italy: 1911–1926

Peter comes to a halt at a gate barring the road. This is a railway crossing. When a train approaches, the cars must wait to let it pass by.

The locomotive whistles and Peter gives a friendly wave as it thunders by.

Gatekeeper's office

Wayside altar

1921 Motoguzzi

Gallant gatekeeper

Telegraph pole

1911 Fiat state landaulette

Italian State Railways express locomotive

Chapel

Olive tree

Fiat 15 Ter military ambulance, 1913

Railway crossing sign

1926 Lancia Lambda

An aerodynamic Alfa of 1913, capable of 90 MPH!

Alfa Romeo "RL Super Sport", 1925

A picnic

Ugly litter

A rusting wreck

GARAG

Citroën "Kegresse" half-track car, 1923

A chassis

Repair workshop

Jack

Railroad crossing sign

Winch

A golfer's driver

1923 Renault desert car

1921 Le Zèbre

Propeller-powered Leyat, 1921

26

. DELOR

"Sputter, Sput, Putt!" coughs
the engine of Peter Pebble's car.
It's nearly out of gas.
Luckily there is a garage nearby,
and Peter turns off the road,
pulling up to the gasoline pumps.
Peter takes a moment to admire
the busy mechanics repairing and
servicing a number of cars.

Office

ESSENCE
TROSHAIR
HUILE

Car wash

Gasoline pumps

Checking the
gas level

Oil
barrel

Air
compressor
pump

Citroën 10CV of 1919

Checking
the
water level

1920 Peugeot

Destination
card

NICE

Hopeful
hitchhiker

A magnificent
Bugatti "Royale"
from about 1927

A nautical-looking
Renault 40 CV
of the 1920s

1926 Amilcar

27

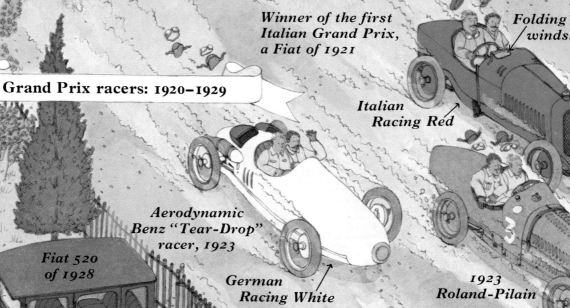

Winner of the first Italian Grand Prix, a Fiat of 1921

Folding windshield

Italian Racing Red

Grand Prix racers: 1920–1929

Aerodynamic Benz "Tear-Drop" racer, 1923

Fiat 520 of 1928

German Racing White

1923 Roland-Pilain

French Racing Blue

Aerodynamic Voisin racer, 1923

Starting handle

1923 Atlantic, Germany

1928 Isotta Fraschini, Italy

1928 Opel 4/18 PS, Germany

The pits

Race official

Filling with gasoline

Coach

Changing a tire

ROMEO F.I

A classic racer the Alfa Romeo P2 of 1924

Jack

Italian for "FINISH"

TRAGUARDO

The checkered flag

Mirror

Stone screen

A winner of many races, the Bugatti 35, 1924–1930

1928 Maserati 26 B

British Racing Green

3-liter Bentley, winner of the Le Mans endurance race of 1927

With a tank full of gasoline, Peter Pebble drives off again with renewed speed.
His car bounces along the grass, and "CRACK!" right through a fence, onto a racetrack.
The checkered flag flutters at the finish line, and it looks as if Peter has taken first place!
Hurrah for Peter!

Stupefied spectators

DATE

FINISH!

*Electric
toy Bugatti, 1930*